PEACE

WORLD PEACE

SPECIFIC THINGS TO DO TO HAVE WORLD PEACE

PART ONE, VOL. 1 (many series coming)

By Prince Gabriel **(Hon. Veteran, US Army)**

Copyright © Prince Gabriel B. Atsepoyi, 2010

Studied Law, LL.B. 1986-1990 (British Legal System), BA History, University of Colorado, Executive MBA, JD Candidate, Boston

INTRODUCTION

If world peace you crave, world peace you shall get.

If national peace you want, national peace you shall

get. If you want peace within yourself or peace with

others, (you must have inner peace before you can

have peace with others, a must!), the peace you so

crave is within reach, my brothers and sisters.

It is very easy to have world peace: we all just need

to come back to nature (<u>with a clean hand</u>, honesty,

sincerity, <u>ready to do justice</u>, fairness and equality),

from whose bosom we all emanated.

If you see a naked man/woman running around naked, with no clothes on, first, you put on your clothes before you run around to help that mad person. If you run around naked, like the mad man/woman, you become a mad person yourself. See that!

However, a mad person running around naked has gone back to nature. Why can't we all get naked publicly and shout and scream, without making any sense like a mad person. In other words please reverse (in a very funny, unique way, I will show you how later) every solution or idea you have used for years that have failed you in getting peace and see what I mean here.

We have lived on this earth for over ten thousand years according to scientific data available everywhere now that it is common knowledge (at least in the Western World). We have tried to make sense of everything but to no avail. The world has never known peace. From the senseless killings of the Jews and others by the Christian Crusades in the 10th and 11th centuries onward to the Islamic Jihads, 9/11 senseless killings, American Civil War (1861-65), World War 1 and World War 11, (1914-

1919 &1939-1945), the Vietnam war, the Korean war, The Gulf Wars, the war in Afghanistan, and so many countless wars and killings going on right now and into the future unabatedly.

Well, some people say "no war is good". Others say "no, war is good". What do you think? Where do you stand in this argument?

I think both sides are correct: sometimes "no war is good"; because peace is necessarily, at all times better than war. While at other times, and in a limited sense, as a matter of last resort (only) to defend yourself or your sovereignty, "no, war is good".

Now, for so many years we have tried to have peace but to no avail. We have tried everything humanely possible, ideas from some of the so-called "best and brightest" people alive (and ideas from the so-called best universities and colleges like Harvard, Yale, Oxford, Cambridge, MIT, etc) yet that elusive word "peace" has not been attained nationally or globally. The reasons for not having peace are as numerous, complex and confusing as almost the same reasons husbands and wives or lovers can no longer get alone, hence the high rate of divorce today. Everyone now wants a nuclear life or a nuclear family of some sort, or a different life, etc. I have given several practical things to do to have *trust, bonding and peace,* in my books (please see The Book of Total Happiness and Secrets of Happy Family, etc).

In this book I am here to propose novel, innovative, and unique ideas for personal peace and/or national peace and/or world peace.

Chapter One

The Clinton Example

Bill and Hilary Clinton just celebrated the marriage of their only daughter, Chelsea (a Christian), to a long-time boy friend, Marc Mezvinsky, Jewish, because Chelsea and Marc are deeply in love with each other! Isn't this the way nature has intended things to be? I think that is in accordance with natural law, equity and good conscience. That is to say: move out of your comfort zone and meet different people on the other side of the isle. If you are rich or wealthy, please marry a poor person and vice versa. It is time too for a woman to become President of the United States and Secretary-General of the United Nations, etc. Please let us *reverse* all the ways we have been handling world problems for us to have everlasting, true and real, peace. Please! The feelings of love, unity, <u>peace</u>, progress, togetherness, and camaraderie can sometimes be exhilarating, just to say the least.

Perhaps leaders of the world like Benjamin Netanyahu (and other leaders in Israel too) should <u>please</u> allow his children to get out of his culture and religion freely and mingle with the Moslems and vice versa; perhaps, something strong and tight might happen. Perhaps a marriage (like Chelsea and Marc) or a deeper bond might seal the disagreements between the Israelis and the Palestinians. It is time to reverse our approach and ideas hitherto, and try the opposites.

In the case of North Korea, Iran, the United States and the rest of the world, perhaps the President of the United States should invite the current Presidents of North Korea and Iran (separately) to the White House for a dinner! Talk heart to heart with people on equal and/or just terms, naturally. Find common ground naturally, meet more frequently, exchange gifts, compromise, while seating face to face, touch each other with permission, become friends forever, seal your friendship with something unbreakable naturally, something as strong and valuable like diamonds, marriage, etc. Come back to nature people! You have all strayed away from nature for too long. Please come back to nature my dear brothers and sisters. I speak to you as nobody, but, please listen to me World Leaders! Please come back to nature and have everlasting Peace. Please!!!

You see, human beings are necessarily good. Whenever you isolate people or tag people or disrespect people (in any form or shape) or oppress people, people are going to act up. I hope somebody is listening. Reverse your tactics please.

Chapter Two

War is a Waste. Use the money to build life...

The billions and trillions of dollars spent in the Gulf

Wars and in Afghanistan and the endless wars in the

world currently could transform the entire

civilization of the world, if the same amount of

money is spent diligently in building schools, roads,

colleges, training teachers, and given freely to all

the poor people in the world to better themselves.

Please let us reverse the current approaches to solving problems as we journey progressively into the future.

The following suggestions should be taken seriously. Please.

1. Instead of Congress declaring war in the United States, the citizens of the United States should be asked first in a referendum to declare war; a 2/3 vote in favor should be required to go to any war in the future. With that 2/3 in favor then Congress can declare war. Natural law

requires every American to be consulted formally before any future war is declared because America is wasting its talents and natural resources through countless, unnecessary wars. Although, I am nobody right now, please listen to me because I served with HONORS in the United States Army. <u>Thank you for listening</u>.

2. We all need to get back to nature and become selfless and happy again. We all need natural love and affection, naturally. Happy and selfless people always do peace. Happy and generous

people will feed the hungry and needy people of the world. Unless we feed the poor and needy people of the world and teach everyone how to fish independently (that is help everyone, help every poor person to become educated, free from diseases, and be financially and economically balanced in life, and then become self-reliant), unless that, there can be no *real* peace.

Below are practical things we can all do to have happiness, selfless life and togetherness with one another and hence <u>peaceful life</u>:

1. Learn to laugh loud daily. Every time you have course to laugh, just laugh as loud as you can if it means you falling down on the ground, crying happily, bouncing your legs and hands- do it! A good laugh well expressed without any kind of restrictions will help your body, spirit and soul to be alive and well. Laughter is the best expression of happiness, no matter your

physical or physiological problems, please laugh, laugh and laugh. Laughter is the best natural medicine to life's tumult. So, laugh away your sorrow. Laugh because you are beautiful. Laugh because life is beautiful. Laugh, laugh...

2. Learn how to sing daily, whether you know how to sing or nor, just sing, sing to people, sing to yourself, sing aloud, sing silently, just sing to yourself. Singing takes so many forms, you can hum, whistle or mime. Please do not let a day go by without singing. Sing, clap your hands...

3. Dancing. Put on your music and dance daily. Put on your favorite music or beat your drums. Whether you listen to music or not just dance daily. The moment you cultivate the habit of dancing daily, the sky is the limit. Please dance in the morning, dance in the afternoon, dance at night even when you are sleeping at night get up and dance! Dance and be lively always!

4. Everyone should fall in love and have a relationship in order to be happy. Do whatever you have to do attract a partner that you can fall in love with. The most important thing is

that you should be thinking daily of somebody you truly like and love. A good friend or good lover that you can tell stories, sing, eat, laugh and go dancing with, a confidant. Every man or woman out there should be falling in love and staying steadfast in love. Try to be passionate on a daily basis it is very, very essential for happiness!

5. Live a natural life on a daily basis, even if for only one hour. Learn to stay without electricity or the microwave, or anything artificial. Enjoy nature, feel the sun, take a walk on the beach,

eat organic foods, stay quiet in the room without any music playing, or sit down and listen to the whistling birds and trees. Feel and enjoy nature more frequently, please.

6. Get involved with a least a sport in your life. It could be football, soccer, tennis, swimming, athletics or golf. Just get busy with a sport or more.

7. Learn the habit of saying "Yes, you can do it" to every dream or goal you have. Whether you are in college or a new profession, tell yourself that

you can be successful. You will be successful!
Trust me.

8. Whenever you come across any sharp object or pins on the ground or floor, pick it up and put it away in a trash. In other words, try to do favors to strangers every time even when no one has asked you, and without expecting anything in return. Be proactive in helping others.

9. Learn something new that you never knew before in your life daily. It could be reading a new book, cooking a new meal, looking up new

information on the internet just learn something new daily.

10.   Surprise a homeless or poor person with a large sum of money without letting your identity known to that person and just walk away, periodically.

11.   Do something nice for children, at least once every week, it could be in the daycare, elementary school, charity or orphanage home just do something for the children, at least once a week.

12. Surprise your mother or an old lady who is in need of help with a special gift at least once a month.

13. Are you getting enough sleep daily? Say six to eight hours of sleep daily. Please relax and cool your mind, body and soul. In order to be truly happy daily, you need all the sleep and rest you can get. You can check with your doctors to verify this important fact of life: please get good sleep, ok! Tips to getting good sleep: first eat good food, get exercise, then a bath, stay in a quiet, dark room, empty your mind of any thoughts, stay blank, relax,

sometime soft classical music on very low

volume, may help, stay quiet...

14. If you ever quarrel with anyone, or if you

have any enemy, learn to make amends as

quickly as possible. Just forgive and forget, even

if it means losing some money or losing face or

if it means you are cheated in some form, do

not worry about it. For, if you let little trifles

bother your life, your enemy has defeated you,

even if you won a case against your enemy, or

even if you are victorious in war or conflict, it

does not matter! Please do not keep a

protracted conflict. Do not keep enemy, period!

The very fundamental tenet of happiness, or

being happy, forbids enemy, period! Please try

this idea and see what I mean. Please apologize,

give in, let go of that thing, and simply move on

to more interesting thing, more rewarding thing

in life, please! As the parable goes: if you see a

naked, mad person running around naked on

the street, do not run after that naked person,

with yourself naked too; if you do, you become

a mad person too! Got it? The message for

some of the very best ways to manage the human affairs is coded in the Itsekiri language, and like many great lessons of wisdom, it cannot be converted into the English Language; so I am just going to say it in Itsekiri thus: ***ogba bi ireh owu agbadueyewe, etsuja ooo!*** I hope all the war mongers out there in America, Afghanistan, Iraq, Iran, North Korean, Israel, the Palestinians, etc, get the message now before it is too late!

Do all these things religiously, besides other things that you consider excellent in life and forget about being happy! (see The Book of Total Happiness)

PERIOD OF FRIENDSHIP OR COURTSHIP

Some dos and Don'ts during Courtship

1. Do not emphasize sex during dates. Especially during the initial period of dating. Please don't!

Why? Well, I will explain the reason in a parable thus: when you are trying to drink your soup with a spoon, make sure that the soup is not too hot or too warm. If it is too hot, it would burn your mouth, and you would not enjoy it, or would you? So, my friend, please cool down, do not be in a rush, take your time before sipping, ok. Second, and most important: make sure you do not drink the soup dripping from the bottom or body of the spoon. Rather, you should be patient and drink the soup that is plentiful inside the spoon, alright. For if you are in a rush and try to drink the soup dripping from outside or around the spoon, the larger quantity of soup inside the spoon will spill or pour away completely, and then, you will be famished! And you will have no soup left to drink! Got it?

2. Don't direct your talk or conversation to sexual topics during the initial phone calls. Also, don't make excessive phone calls. Please be moderate.

3. Don't swear

4. Don't devote too much time to talking about yourself or your qualities. Talk less. Listen

more. Do humor. Do lots of clean humors! Be natural. Let your prospective mate take time to know you, sometime, with little or no help from you, alright. So relax my friend.

5. Don't interrupt when he/she is talking. Take turns. Be tactful.

6. Don't try to take total control of the conversation. Be social. Be reasonable.

7. Always ask for feedback and how you can better yourself next time, and please follow-up with any suggestion. Improve yourself daily.

DO's

8. Do let your prospective mate know how genuinely interested you are.

9. Do give hints about places and things of interest.

10. Do attend carefully to conversation. Be interesting. Be real. Be amiable.

11. Do humor. Yes, you can! If you lack jokes, watch comedy shows, ok.

12. Do honesty, be conscientious and modest.

13. Do stay neat and dress up at all times, visit the dentist more often now.

14. Do learn all table manners for restaurants. Exhibit good manners.

15. Do get good sleep before your date, smile always and be happy.

16. **WHAT TO SAY:** "Please", when you ask him or her to help you or give you something

17. "Thank you", to him or her after they have helped you or or give you something

18. "Excuse me" or "Pardon me" when you interrupt, burp, fart the air, or accidentally bump into someone

19. "I'm sorry", when you do something that hurts or bothers someone

20. "Hello" or "How do you do?" when greeting him or her. When parting company say: "Good Bye. It was really nice to meet you".

21. **ON SPECIFIC OCCASIONS:** when eating, keep your elbows off the table; put your napkin on your lap; chew with your mouth

closed. Don't tip back in your chair. Don't

complain about the food. Ask to be excused.

And help with the dishes, if appropriate.

22. During a performance, be quiet. Afterward,

clap as a gesture of appreciation. When

calling someone on the phone, say, "Hello.

This is ...May I please speak with..." When

answering the phone, say "Hello. May I ask

who is calling?"

23. When people come to visit, invite them in,

offer them a seat, juice or water and treat

them courteously. If someone sends you a

present, express your thanks or gratitude in a call or a note. Thus, always observe ethical conduct; be simplistic, hospitable and considerate.

24. Know thyself. Know your friend. Spend time with anyone you consider your friend or lover and get to know him/her. It is a period of discovery. However, be careful. There are certain things you should know; there are certain things that you should not know. Please do not talk too much about the past nasty things. The reason being that you do

not want to foul your house or home with your stinking mouth or excreta, especially, when all the doors and windows are closed; unless you enjoy eating your own shit! Yak! Please, let peace reign always. Be creative and innovative. Make your friend or lover laugh and happy always, and not sad, ok.

25. However, do not close your eyes to unpleasant facts during courtship, as you will certainly face them after your marriage or during a long term relationship. Be tactful in discussing things. Talk less. Listen more. And

respect each other's opinions, no matter how silly or stupid. Everything is valid.

26. No relationship is perfect, and none should strive to be perfect. Just be natural. Take life easy and do not let a day pass you by without saying something good or finding something good about your friend or spouse. Each person must question themselves what they expect out of this relationship. Your physical needs, like great sex, with multiple orgasms for the girl/woman daily (!) or weekly. The best techniques for the best sex coming your

way shortly, ok! Other needs include emotional needs, religious needs, etc. Please do not be shy. Please do not delay or procrastinate in discussing these things. Please. Just be polite and be respectful in talking about anything, that's all!

27. Whatever you sow, you shall reap eventually. So, please sow something excellent, do something outstanding now so that at the time of harvest you will have reason to be happy, happy, happy...forever! For instance, go to college or university and

learn a solid profession (law, medicine, accounting, engineering, etc) and once you find your niche in life, let it be something that is outstanding in nature that you are very happy doing yourself; and a trade or profession that would also bring you respect and dignity in your life, got it?

28. Be interested in each other. Talk about each other's interests and offer advice without dictating anything. Do not criticize openly, but disagree lovingly and in a friendly manner. Touch each other during disagreement and

keep the oil in your lamp burning always; let

your lamp keep burning and shining forever,

alright!

29. Meet with the parent of your friend. Talk

less. Listen more. Do shores while there.

Show good attitude; however, talk briefly

about your short comings or weakness in life.

Be honest. Be natural. Be generous.

30. Learn to cook. Learn to cook for each other.

Learn each other's favorite meal and surprise

each other always. Good relationship that

endures forever is about *quid pro quo,* or give and take. That is what life is about anyway.

31. Money is perhaps the biggest issue in any relationship. Please get solid profession or trade or training in life, work very, very hard for money and, please enjoy yourself daily. Everyone is born to be rich and wealthy. No one is born to be poor. You just need to get out and get your share of the millions out there legally. Albeit, you do not have to be rich or wealthy to be happy, but it would help greatly, if you have regular income, trust me!

Be a hustler, make money, lots of it, if you lucky, share with others if you want to be happy, and just have great time with your friend and family. Just enjoy life daily while it lasts. Take wine to gladden the heart, eat good meal, balanced diet, with lots of fruits and vegetables and drink water daily. Please do everything in *moderation.*

If you do not have money, don't worry, keep working hard, go to college or university or read books, all the formulas and answers you need to succeed in life are in books. Trust me!

Sleep in the library, if possible, read all the books in a good library (and keep notes and journals of your discoveries) until you get the magic formulas or answers to make lots of money, ok!

32. Watch out for your weight. Please walk out daily and exercise, exercise, exercise...every minute, every hour, every day, please!!! You cannot be happy in life without a regular exercise to stay agile, keep body, spirit and soul active and lively and stay healthy! Exercise on a daily basis, like cleaning your

home, having great sex and sweating profusely every time, and walking out or running, and so on; exercise is to happiness, what honey is to life. In fact, exercise is the like the salt in our food, without which life is tasteless!

33. Finally, keep the counsel or friendship of older couples who are successful in marriage or in a long term relationship. Listen to them and copy some good things you notice from them. But, be unique and original in your approach to your relationship and your

future. Map out your own life, improve your

styles and your models daily, stay alert on the

wheel in your journey to the future fraught

with tumults, and refine your lives and add

spices to it; enjoy your life like there is no

tomorrow, save lots of money in the bank or

under your pillow if you choose; just save lots

of money for rainy days; invest widely in

different portfolios, share your wealth with

the poor and needy, and for goodness sake

enjoy good sex and good wine, in your

relentless pursuit of happiness!

Chapter Three

People Swap, in a Super-Continent

Just imagine for a moment that once a year all the

poor people in poor countries are swapped with all

the rich people in rich countries, for sort of a role

play! Wouldn't that be fun!

Or, let's say all the members of the Taliban and *al*

Qaeda are allowed free tickets in a first class seat to

fly to the United States and Europe; and while there

these people are given free tickets to Disney World

and/or Disney Land, treated to a life of affluence

and enjoyment, free cruise around the world, the

finest of wine and beautiful girls in bikinis are

provided free of charge; in short all the best things

in life are provided free of charge for these people!

And while these Taliban people are away on free

holidays in the Western World their countries are

turned into heaven on earth, roads well constructed

and paved like in London or in the United States,

schools are built, every part of the city and town is

well planned and constructed, free homes are built

for all the people, and at least one billion dollars is provided in cash money free of charge for all the people to start a new life and better their lives! Could somebody please try my panacea here and see wonders working and everlasting peace once and forever, for the first time ever. Please! And please don't ask me where the money for this endless enjoyment for the people on the other side of the isle is coming from. We only need less that 1% of the trillions we are currently wasting in endless wars around the globe to treat these people to great life and permanent enjoyment and change their thinking and ideology for good. Well, if we are serious about *World Peace* this is a panacea that is natural, practical and realistic. Please hear me out my dear brothers and sisters out there. Please listen to me World Leaders! The world cannot go on like this peacefully! Everything is unnatural, please people! We need to adopt my idea of "people swap" in a super-continental system, where people end up in role play: the rich should endure some poverty for few weeks/months, while all the poor people should move into the homes of the rich. That's natural! That is one of the best ways to everlasting peace! During the role play the poor and the rich should be allowed to take whatever she/he likes and keep all the things she/he is able to carry away. Wouldn't that be wonderful, people! Isn't that the way nature has decreed this life to be?!

Please tell me any better ways to resolve inequality, injustice, oppression and hence lack of peace in this world! Please tell me, I am listening!

Other Books by Gabriel B. Atsepoyi or Prince Gabriel

1. *The Book of Total Happiness*

2. *Jungle of Confusion*

3. *How to have good sex and be happy forever in your relationship*

4. *The ultimate Leadership and Management techniques for the 21st Century and beyond: Ultimate management styles to bring everyone on board*

5. *The Poor Man: The Poor versus The Rich. How to make it from Rags to Riches*

6. *The Complete works of Gabriel B. Atsepoyi*

7. *Effective and Efficient Ways to Managing Nigeria in the21st century and beyond*

8. *An American Soldier Protesting Bad Treatment to Women, Children & The Poor*

9. *Funny Stories. Laugh & Laugh*

10. *A cow boy who lost his wife*

11. *Family & Security from Thief*

12. *Safety for Kids: Fun Programs to prevent crimes & make youths productive*

13. *Special Gifts for you*

14. *Secrets of Happy Family: Practical things to do to unite & have fun!*

15. *Sex Me (Ultimate sex techniques)*

16. *How to be a great leader and a great Manager, both at work & at Home (Part One)*

17. *How to be a great leader and a great Manager, both at work & at Home (Part Two)*

18. *How to be a great leader and a great Manager, both at work & at Home (Part Three)*

19. *How to be a great leader and a great Manager, both at work & at Home (Part Four)*

20. *How to be a great leader and a great Manager, both at work & at Home (Part Five)*

21. *How to be a great leader and a great Manager, both at work & at Home (Part Six)*

22. *How to be a great leader and a great Manager, both at work & at Home (Part Seven)*

23. *How to be a great Manager and a great Leader, both at work & at Home (Part Eight)*

24. *How be a great Manager and a great Leader, both at work & at Home (Part Nine)*

25. *How be a great Manager and a great Leader, both at work & at Home (Part Ten)*

26. *How be a great Manager and a great Leader, both at work & at Home (Vols. 1-10)*

27. *Catholic Sex Scandal: Is it time to dissolve the Catholic Church...? Part One*

28. *Catholic Sex Scandal: Can a woman become a Pope to save the Church? Part two*

29. *Catholic Church Sex Scandal: Please Forgive the Catholic Church, Part three*

30. *How to lose weight quickly. Best methods like in the US Army, Part one*

31. A Letter from an American Soldier to all poor people in the world: come to America for

your survival...come, come, come...

32. When sex and soccer meets. How to score a goal with your lover

33.   RAW MEAT IN KIDS BURGER
RAW MEAT SERVED TO KIDS AT CARL'S JR IN AURORA, COLORADO

Part 1, Vol. 1

34. PEACE. WORLD PEACE. Specific things to do to have world peace. Part 1, Vol. 1

This is Gabriel Atsepoyi, an American Soldier. He studied Law (LL.B), BA History, MBA and a Doctorate Degrees in Management. (Univ of Colorado, Cambridge, etc). **If you have special talent and you want sponsorship to the USA or any country, please get in touch with me pronto**. You can also consult me for Leadership ideas, and ways to improve any government or corporation. I **am ready and able to help the USA Government or Nigeria Government anytime. Please call me! 720 934 1983 USA.**

CONTACT ME ANYTIME: Gabriel.atsepoyi@yahoo.com Or gatsepoyi@gmail.com

Prince.gabriell@gmail.com**, or,** atsepoyi@hotmail.com

Telephone number in the United States: 720 934 1983

Or write to me regarding any other business you wish to do with me, like Wealth Management, Partnerships, or any issue, etc. Send your letters to:

Gabriel B. Atsepoyi

Doctorate program

5775 DTC BLVD, SUITE 100

GREENWOOD VILLAGE, COLORADO 80111 USA

FAX 303 694 6673

THE BOOK OF TOTAL HAPPINESS
by Gabriel B. Atsepoyi (Akpieyi)

Education is the key to learning any subject better, so why should it be any different when it comes to being happy? This is the premise for Gabriel Atsepoyi's *The Book of Total Happiness*, in which the author gives new meaning to the search for happiness and contentment in one's life.

It has been said that psychological maturity is achieved when one gains a secure understanding of the meaning of life and one's place in it. This fascinating volume explores this matter in full detail concerning happiness, marriage, health and physical well-being. Regardless of religious or philosophical persuasion, readers will become engrossed in this presentation, which to its credit does not intend to talk down to readers, but instead provides working guidelines in a straightforward and easily understood fashion.

Given the high rate of divorce these days, Mr. Atsepoyi believes that without some form of education concerning marriage, the do's and don't's, the expectations and the compromises, people are destined to continue to allow this shocking statistic to grow. This book's goal, therefore, is to begin that education, to provide understandable paths toward that elusive spiritual habitat, being happy. It's not as easy as it seems, says the author, and most people have to work at it. Yet, it is not totally out of reach, if one can look at life with honest appraisal and work to change those things that hinder one's happiness.

One of the more intriguing aspects of this book is the point that not everyone achieves the same level of happiness, nor has the same avenues available to them in their search for personal happiness. That is fine, says the author, because no two people are exactly the same. Each must find that place that is comfortable for him or her, then work to maintain those good feelings through effort and commitment.

Mr. Atsepoyi's prose is fluid and expressive, and his observations are shrewdly punctuated by a basic wisdom that will appeal to all. But what makes this book be singled out from the many is the significant contribution it makes toward re-educating people of the how and why of being happy. This serves a most practical purpose, first in helping the reader to find paths and guidelines for being happy, the author is also boldly illustrating the power of individual expression, positive thinking, and having a goal to work toward.

Highly recommended for its insight and analyses, *The Book of Total Happiness*, by Gabriel Atsepoyi, is must reading. The author's ideas are lucid and innovative, portraying much wisdom and common sense, and combining all these attributes into one volume enables each reader to further his or her education on perhaps the most important subject matter existing today, the art of being happy.

Section Two of the book focuses on: A-Z about HIV/AIDS and the latest facts on AIDS, protection for kids and family, women's rights (the need to respect and protect women), smoking and its hazards, environmental protection/prevention, how and the need for better education for children, etc., etc.

THE BOOK OF TOTAL HAPPINESS

ABOUT THE AUTHOR

Gabriel Atsepoyi (Akpieyi), twenty-six years old, was born in Africa and presently resides in Colorado.

An avid reader, Mr. Atsepoyi makes it known that the only way he is happy is when he is helping others. His love of God serves his existence well, as he expands upon his belief that one's knowledge is one's power in leading a happy and successful life.

A member of the Optimist Club of Arvada, the author has had many articles published previously on a variety of topics, yet his overriding concerns are for the rate of divorce and its effects toward broken homes, unhappy families, neglected children, uneducated and uncultured children, and crime. He has propounded many solutions in these areas in his latest work, and his hope is that readers will reflect upon those suggestions.

11-24-99
7am-9am
New York
U.S.A.

THE BOOK OF TOTAL HAPPINESS
by Gabriel B. Atsepoyi (Akpieyi)

Education is the key to learning any subject better, so why should it be any different when it comes to being happy? This is the premise for Gabriel Atsepoyi's *The Book of Total Happiness*, in which the author gives new meaning to the search for happiness and contentment in one's life.

It has been said that psychological maturity is achieved when one gains a secure understanding of the meaning of life and one's place in it. This fascinating volume explores this matter in full detail concerning happiness, marriage, health and physical well-being. Regardless of religious or philosophical persuasion, readers will become engrossed in this presentation, which to its credit does not intend to talk down to readers, but instead provides working guidelines in a straightforward and easily understood fashion.

Given the high rate of divorce these days, Mr. Atsepoyi believes that without some form of education concerning marriage, the do's and don't's, the expectations and the compromises, people are destined to continue to allow this shocking statistic to grow. This book's goal, therefore, is to begin that education, to provide understandable paths toward that elusive spiritual habit, being happy. It's not as easy as it seems, says the author, and most people have to work at it, but it is not totally out of reach, if one can look at life with honest appraisal and work to change those things that hinder one's happiness.

One of the more intriguing aspects of the book is the point that not everyone achieves the same level of happiness, nor has the same avenues available to them in their search for personal happiness. That is fine, says the author, because no two people are exactly the same. Each must fine that place that is comfortable for him or her, then work to maintain those good feelings through effort and commitment.

Mr. Atsepoyi's prose is fluid and expressive, and his observations are shrewdly punctuated by a basic wisdom that will appeal to all. But what makes this book be singled out from the many is the significant contribution it makes toward re-educating people of the how and why of being happy. This serves a most practical purpose, first in helping the reader to find paths and guidelines for being happy, the author is also boldly illustrating the power of individual expression, positive thinking, and having a goal to work toward.

Highly recommended for its insight and analy-

ses, *The Book of Total Happiness*, by Gabriel Atsepoyi, is must reading. The author's ideas are lucid and innovative, portraying much wisdom and common sense, and combining all these attributes into one volume enables each reader to further his or her education on perhaps the most important subject matter existing today, the art of being happy.

Section Two of the book focuses on: A-Z about HIV/AIDS and the latest facts on AIDS, protection for kids and family, women's rights (the need to respect and protect women), smoking and its hazards, environmental protection/prevention, how and the need for better education for children, etc., etc.

THE BOOK OF TOTAL HAPPINESS

ABOUT THE AUTHOR

Gabriel Atsepoyi (Akpieyi), twenty-six years old, was born in Africa and presently resides in Colorado.

An avid reader, Mr. Atsepoyi makes it known that the only way he is happy is when he is helping others. His love of God serves his existence well and he expands upon his belief that one's knowledge is one's power in leading a happy and successful life.

A member of the Optimist Club of Arvada, the author has had many articles published previously on a variety of topics, yet his overriding concerns are for the rate of divorce and its effects toward broken homes, unhappy families, neglected children, uneducated and uncultured children, and crime. He has propounded many solutions in these areas in his latest work, and his hope is that readers will reflect upon those suggestions.

ISBN 0-963695-0-X

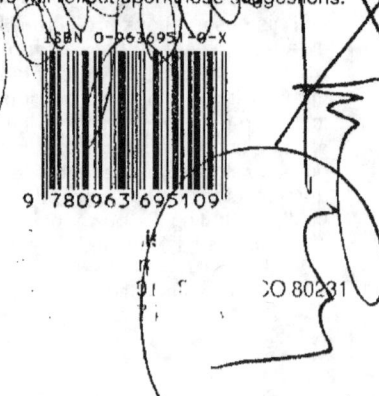

9 780963 695109

CO 80231

Intentionally left blank

Take good care of yourself, eat nutritionally balanced diet, lots of fruits and vegetables, and drink lots of water daily, exercise daily, please fall in love have good sex more frequently, keep good friends who are ready to be educated and work hard in life to enjoy their lives, be friendly with everyone regardless of race, gender, ethnicity, greed or religion, make everyone your friend and your family, give to the poor always, help the needy always, be the first to say hello to friends and strangers, be smart and stay away from trouble always, talk less, listen more, better yourself daily, improve your life daily, forgive always, respect and protect girls and women always, laugh daily and be around happy people, do humor, take life easy, enjoy life while it lasts, go out and get the millions of dollars waiting for you, since no one is born to be poor, get education and seek information daily, be rich in morality, do those things that are excellent, and have lots, and lots of fun! Bye!

Intentionally left blank

OPRAH
THE OPRAH WINFREY SHOW

August 20, 1993

Mr. Gabriel B. Atsepoyi
8826 E. Florida Ave. #101
Denver, CO 80231

Dear Mr. Atsepoyi,

It was such a delight to receive your book Total
Happiness. I am grateful. Your kindness and
thoughtfulness are appreciated.

Again, thank you for thinking of me.

Best wishes,

Oprah Winfrey

OW:sb

P O BOX 909715
CHICAGO ILLINOIS 60690

Can you give hope to others? Can you help to make hope realistic? Can you help to make good things to happen in other people's lives? Can you? Could you please try? Please.

<u>Thank you.</u>

www.ingramcontent.com/pod-product-compliance
Lightning Source LLC
Chambersburg PA
CBHW08141528052б

45788CB00009B/3107